Animal Brainiacs

VICKY FRANCHINO

Children's Press®
An Imprint of Scholastic Inc.

Content Consultant
Dr. Stephen S. Ditchkoff
Professor of Wildlife Sciences
Auburn University
Auburn, Alabama

Library of Congress Cataloging-in-Publication Data
Franchino, Vicky, author.
 Animal brainiacs / Vicky Franchino.
    pages cm. — (A true book)
 Summary: "Discover which animal species have the best memories, which ones are the best
at solving problems, and how these creatures use their remarkable intelligence to thrive in the
wild"— Provided by publisher.
 Includes bibliographical references and index.
 ISBN 978-0-531-21543-2 (library binding) — ISBN 978-0-531-21580-7 (pbk.)
1. Animal intelligence—Juvenile literature. 2. Animal behavior—Juvenile literature. I. Title.
II. Series: True book.
 QL785.F68 2016
 591.5'13—dc23   2014049197

Front cover: A dog ridng a bike
Back cover: Young chimpanzees playing

Find the Truth!

Everything you are about to read is true *except* for one of the sentences on this page.

Which one is **TRUE**?

T or F   Many animals use tools.

T or F   Smarter animals have bigger brains.

Find the answers in this book.

3

Contents

THE BIG TRUTH!

Animal Brains

Jaybird

Sperm whales use a language of clicks to communicate.

4 Learning About Animal Intelligence

Why might a scientist study an animal in the field rather than in a lab? **37**

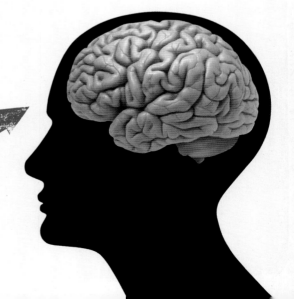

The human brain is roughly 75 percent water.

CHAPTER 1

Animals Can Do Amazing Things!

The branches of a tree are covered with clusters of orange and black. Are these colorful flowers? No, look closer—they are monarch butterflies! These delicate creatures have stopped for a rest. They are on a journey from the northern United States to their winter home in Mexico. Scientists are not sure how monarchs know when to travel south. Experts think day length and temperature could be responsible.

 Monarch butterflies travel hundreds or thousands of miles to their winter home.

Following Their Instincts

Animals often do things that seem astonishing. Monarch butterflies fly south. Spiders know how to spin a web as soon as they are born. Bears hibernate to survive the brutal cold of winter. Newly hatched sea turtles march to the sea and swim until they reach a protective patch of sea grass. Are these signs that these animals are very smart? No, they are just following their instincts.

Sea turtles return to the same beach where they were born, to lay their eggs.

Honeyguides may lead humans to beehives. After the humans crack open a hive and take the honey, the honeyguide enjoys the wax and young bees left behind.

Instinct vs. Intelligence

Instinct is something an animal is born with, not something it learns. All animals use their instincts, including humans. Babies know to cry to get someone's attention. No one has to teach them!

Intelligence means animals can watch the world around them, learn about it, and change their behavior to accomplish tasks. Being able to communicate and remember are also signs of intelligence.

It is very unusual, and a sign of intelligence, if an animal knows itself in a mirror.

Just Like Humans

Sometimes we say an animal is "smart" because it can do things that humans do. Some animals figure out how to make and use tools. Others can copy another animal's actions.

Some animals understand human language. Trainers have taught dolphins and dogs to recognize human symbols and gestures. If you have ever met a pet parrot, it probably knew some human words.

Animals Have Feelings, Too

Emotions are another sign of intelligence. Elephants grieve when a member of their herd dies. They show joy when a baby is born or when they meet up with long-lost relatives.

Chimpanzees can laugh when tickled. Many dog owners believe they have seen their dog smile. Also, have you ever noticed that your pet seems to know when you are especially happy or upset?

Two young chimpanzees laugh and play together.

Special Abilities

Animals have many abilities that humans do not. Some animals can change their coloring to hide from a predator. Certain sea creatures can tell how far away another animal is—and the animal's size—with **echolocation**. They send out an audio signal and can learn about the other animal based on how the sound bounces back.

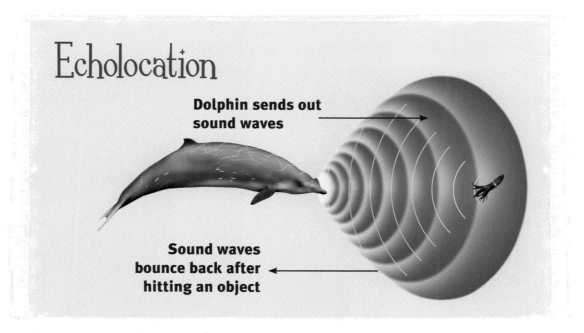

Echolocation

Dolphin sends out sound waves

Sound waves bounce back after hitting an object

Jays have been known to pretend to hide food to confuse other birds.

Animal Tricksters

Animals can be sneaky. Opossums and hognose snakes pretend to be dead if a predator is too close. If they fool the predator, they might escape!

Squirrels bury **caches** of food to prepare for winter. They know other squirrels will try to steal the food. To stop these thieves, a squirrel might pretend to bury food, then hide it somewhere else.

Meerkats take turns
watching for danger.

14

CHAPTER 2

Forests, Fields, and Farms

Both wild and tame animals can be smart. Meerkats send lookouts to protect the mob, or group of meerkats, from danger. Polar bears teach their cubs how to survive in the frigid tundra. Foxes have learned how to thrive in the wilderness and in the city.

Think about the tricks you have taught your pets. What about tricks they have taught themselves? These are signs of intelligence.

Two elephants greet each other.

Elephants Have Good Memories

Have you heard the saying "An elephant never forgets"? It is true! Elephants can remember one another for a long time. Two elephants have been known to recognize each other after 20 years apart.

During a drought in Africa, some older elephants remembered where they had found food during another drought 30 years earlier. The elephants led their herd to this area and saved them.

Barnyard Genius

Do you think pigs are just dirty, lazy animals? They are actually quite tidy and very smart. They only roll in mud to cool off. When they have a choice, the areas they use for a bathroom and for eating are separate.

Pigs can learn to do tricks and solve problems. They can even play video games!

People use pigs to find a very expensive mushroom called a truffle.

Man's Best Friend Is One Smart Beast

For thousands of years, humans have known dogs are smart. They have trained dogs to herd animals and look for lost people.

Dogs can learn tricks and follow commands. They have good memories and are excellent problem solvers. Dogs are also very protective and affectionate.

A dog can be trained to use its natural intelligence in ways that help humans.

Chickens establish a ranking system, called a pecking order, so the flock knows who is in charge.

Henhouse Smarts

Chickens are the smartest of the barnyard animals. They know and recognize hundreds of other chickens. They can also make more than 30 different sounds. Some sounds mean, "Hurry, there is food." Others mean, "Watch out! Danger!"

A lead chicken will let the rest of the flock know it is the boss. This chicken will peck less important chickens if they do not show respect.

This chimpanzee uses a stick to help it drink, after poking the stick into a hole in a rock to soak up water inside.

Our Closest Relatives

It is no surprise that apes are smart. After all, 98 percent of their **DNA** is the same as that found in humans. DNA is like a computer code inside an animal's cells. It affects everything from an animal's height to its health.

Apes are good at many of the same things humans are. They can make and use tools. They live in family groups. Mother apes care for their children and mourn if they die.

Problem Solvers

Chimpanzees are very good at solving problems. Chimps can also copy one another. This might sound easy, but copying is quite uncommon and the sign of a very smart animal. Chimps are even better than humans at one thing: memory games.

Chimpanzees can memorize patterns almost instantly.

A chimpanzee takes a test on its ability to recognize photos.

21

Not Just Pests

Rats can show empathy, which means understanding another rat's feelings. Scientists did an experiment. They trapped one rat and put a piece of chocolate next to it, outside the trap. Another rat was let into the area. This "free" rat could choose to eat the chocolate immediately, but it usually freed the trapped rat first.

Rats are intelligent enough to be trained. This rat is learning how to sniff out dangerous explosives.

Using Tools

Humans create and use tools for a huge range of tasks. However, humans are not the only creatures who do this. Sea otters open a shellfish with a stone. Dolphins protect their nose with a sea sponge. Bonobos use tools to dig, scrape, and break logs. Chimps "fish" for termites with a stick. Orangutans (right) "wear" leaves like gloves or a rain hat.

Animal Brains

Intelligent animals have brains that are divided into sections that do different jobs. Some sections control body parts. Others deal with emotions, learning, problem solving, and memory.

Size matters, too. The more surface area a brain has, the more space there is to hold neurons. Neurons are the cells that send and receive information between the brain and the body. Animals with more neurons can do more.

However, the apparent size of a brain is not everything. A tiny rat, with its small-looking brain, can be just as smart as a big dog with a much bigger brain. How can this be true? Folds! An animal's brain, like a human's, is made up of folded material. The folds provide more space for neurons.

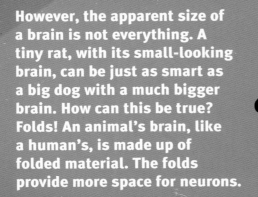

Compare two balls of the same size. One ball should have smooth sides. Make the other ball by crumpling up a piece of paper. When you spread out the materials that form each ball, you'll see that the paper ball has much more surface area than the smooth ball. That larger surface area can hold more neurons than the smooth, smaller surface area.

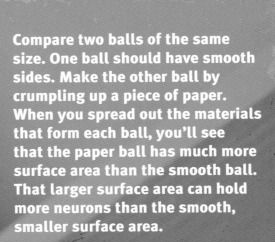

CHAPTER 3

Under the Sea and Up in the Air

In the 1950s, a scientist named John C. Lilly studied dolphins. He believed dolphins were similar to humans in their intelligence and ability to communicate. Today, scientists still believe dolphins are very smart but that their intelligence is less like a human's and more **unique** to dolphins. Scientists also believe dolphins might not be any smarter than a number of other animals.

Dolphins have their own language, plus they can learn complicated commands in a human language.

Scientists still have much more to learn about the massive sperm whale.

Whale Talk

Sperm whales use a sort of "Morse code" language of clicks to talk to one another. Researchers believe that family groups communicate in their own **dialect**. Groups might even have their own "accent" depending on where they live.

It is very challenging to study whales. Most cannot be kept in **captivity,** and it is expensive and difficult to study them at sea.

Many Arms and Many Brains

Octopuses can navigate mazes, learn from one another, and open a jar. They also camouflage themselves by changing their shape, color, or behavior to either blend into the background or scare off a predator. They can also use a shell for a hiding place.

Octopuses are tricky, too! They have even been known to sneak aboard a fishing boat and steal the crew's dinner.

The octopus has nine brains—a central one and one at the end of each arm.

Clever Crows

Crows are good problem solvers. A crow named Betty amazed her trainers when she bent a piece of wire into a hook that she used to get food. It was the first time she had seen wire.

Crows sometimes drop nuts onto a crosswalk. Cars run over the nuts and break the shells. During a red light, the crow swoops down to grab the unshelled nuts for lunch!

Crows have learned a number of clever ways to crack open a nut's hard outer shell, such as dropping them from heights.

Humans have found that ravens are smart enough to be trained.

Remarkable Ravens

Ravens also have a reputation for being smart. In fact, in the 1950s, the U.S. government gave these animals special assignments. Animal trainers taught ravens to set a rock carefully on a windowsill, then fly away. But it was no ordinary rock. It had a secret compartment that hid a special transmitter. When spies met nearby, the transmitter would send their conversation to a government agency.

Alex the African gray parrot called cake "yummy bread."

African grays and other parrots are often curious and intelligent birds.

Parrots

For more than 20 years, researcher Irene Pepperberg worked with an African gray parrot named Alex. She taught Alex to identify colors, numbers, shapes, and words. Alex could do basic math and understand the meanings of "same" and "different."

Other researchers as well have proved parrots are clever. African grays can learn if a box is empty by shaking it. Parrots have also shown they understand it is good to share.

Busy Bees

Life in a bee colony is very complex. Each bee has its own role. It must work with other bees to make sure the hive runs smoothly.

Some bees must know which plants to pollinate and how to find them. When a bee finds nectar and pollen, it shares the good news with other bees by doing a special dance.

A honeybee watches as another bee dances out the location of nectar.

Working Together

Ants are extremely good at a very difficult task: navigation. They use many cues from nature, including wind direction, ground texture, and where the sun is in the sky. They are also very good at working together to solve a problem. When one ant finds food, it leaves a scent trail between the food and the nest. Other ants can follow this path.

Ants work together when they need to travel.

Communication

Lions roar. Elephants trumpet. Whales click. Chickens crow and cluck.

All animals have special ways to "talk" to one another. They often use noises or smells to share information. Scientists are just beginning to understand animal communication.

Some animals have also learned to communicate using human language. One is a gorilla named Koko. Koko knows more than 1,000 words in sign language and about 2,000 words in spoken English.

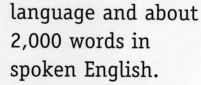

Search and rescue teams use specially trained dogs to find lost people.

CHAPTER 4

Learning About Animal Intelligence

Animals and humans have many things in common. This is not surprising—humans *are* animals! But it is important not to **anthropomorphize** animals. They are not human, and they might have different reasons than humans do for acting a certain way.

Animals have their own types of intelligence, too. Their unique intelligence helps them solve problems in their particular ecosystem and live in conditions where humans could not survive. It also helps animals swim in the water and fly through the air.

Researchers use waterproof touch-screen computers for dolphins.

In the Lab

Many animal studies happen in a laboratory. In labs, researchers can use large or delicate equipment that cannot be taken into the field.

Specialized equipment, such as touch-screen computers, can be important when studying animal intelligence. If a researcher has to help an animal use equipment, test results could change. But an animal can operate a touch screen by itself. This makes findings more accurate. Researchers have used touch screens with turtles, pigeons, dogs, macaques, and dolphins.

Brain Imaging

Researchers in Washington wanted to learn if crows had memories. To do this, they wore masks and caught the crows. This was scary for the birds.

Later, in the lab, the researchers took scans, or pictures, of each bird's brain as the crows were shown the masks. The scans showed, by lighting up, which part of the crow's brain was working. When the crows saw the scary masks, the part of the brain that processes memory lit up in the scan. The crows remembered their experience!

A researcher watches a raven as it works through a problem during an experiment.

Issues in the Lab

Some animal experts are concerned that studies in the lab are artificial, or fake. Animals in a lab behave differently than they would in the wild. They don't need to find food or protect themselves from predators. They could feel depressed or bored because they are not living in their natural **habitat**. All these things could affect the lab results.

Animal research that takes place inside a lab can be beneficial, but it also has limitations.

A researcher films a humpback whale mother and her young in the ocean off the coast of Hawaii.

In the Field

How can we study animals in their natural environment? Sometimes, scientists use tiny cameras. They might attach one to an animal or put the camera in a certain place to film animals in that area. Other times, researchers watch animals in person. They might leave the animals alone and observe their typical activities. Or, researchers may change something in the environment to see how the animals react to that change.

Elephants need to use their trunks to find and reach food.

Do Not Make Assumptions!

Assumptions are things a person believes without proof. Scientists once assumed elephants could not use tools. They tried giving elephants a stick to use to get out-of-reach food. The elephants failed. Then the scientists realized that elephants need their sense of smell. If they pick up a stick with their trunk, then they cannot use the trunk to smell. When the scientists provided a box instead, the elephants stepped on it to reach the food. They could use tools after all!

How Should We Treat Animals?

Animals are smart and have emotions, so some people are against keeping them in zoos and water parks. Many people are concerned that animals suffer in labs. Others argue that zoos and labs are useful, as some animals are **extinct** in the wild but survive in captivity. Also, when we study and interact with animals, we learn how they think and act. We can then figure out how to help them in the wild and perhaps ensure their survival.

What do you think? ★

Many animals are born and raised in captivity.

Intelligence level of the average crow: About the same as a seven-year-old human

Number of words the average dog can learn: 165

Number of faces a sheep can recognize: 50

Number of scent receptors a dog has vs. a human: About 220 million vs. about 5 million

Weight of the average human brain: 3.1 lb. (1.4 kg)

How long humans have been training elephants to do tasks: Thousands of years

Number of types of animals that are extinct in the wild but being raised in captivity: 33

Did you find the truth?

T Many animals use tools.

F Smarter animals have bigger brains.

Resources

Books

dé la Bédoyère, Camilla. *Smartest and Silliest*. Buffalo, NY: Firefly Books, 2011.

Parker, Steve. *Extreme Animals*. Hauppauge, NY: Barrons Educational Series, Inc., 2009.

Rockwood, Leigh. *Chimpanzees Are Smart!* New York: PowerKids Press, 2010.

Visit this Scholastic Web site for more information on animal brainiacs:
★ www.factsfornow.scholastic.com
Enter the keywords **Animal Brainiacs**

Important Words

anthropomorphize (an-thruh-puh-MAWR-phize) — to give animals human forms or characteristics

caches (KASH-iz) — something hidden or stored in a hiding place, especially in the ground

captivity (kap-TIV-i-tee) — the condition of being held or trapped by people

dialect (DYE-uh-lekt) — a way a language is spoken in a particular place or among a particular group

DNA (dee-en-AY) — the molecule found inside every cell in the body, containing information on how each cell should work

echolocation (eh-koh-loh-KAY-shuhn) — process of using sound waves to locate the position of objects in the water

extinct (ik-STINGKT) — no longer found alive

habitat (HAB-uh-tat) — place where an animal or a plant is usually found

intelligence (in-TEL-i-juhns) — the ability to understand, think, and learn

neurons (NOOR-ahnz) — cells that carry information between the brain and other parts of the body

unique (yoo-NEEK) — being the only one of its kind; unlike anything else

Index

Page numbers in **bold** indicate illustrations.

About the Author

Vicky Franchino was extremely surprised to learn that chickens are smart! Her family used to have backyard chickens, and all evidence pointed to them being rather stupid. Franchino has written many books about animals and was fascinated to learn how smart our furry, scaly, and feathered friends truly are. She lives in Madison, Wisconsin, with her family and no pets (even though her youngest daughter would really, really like a dog!).